SACRED

Steve Wheeler

First published by
Wheelsong Books
4 Willow Close, Plymouth PL3 6EY, United Kingdom

First published in 2020

Print ISBN: 979-8-66957-680-6

—

For NRW

Thank you

My grateful thanks go to my friends and to all of my family who in their various ways have inspired me to write this collection of poems.

My eternal thanks go to a king I happen to know personally, and as you read through these poems, perhaps you might also get to know Him.

Steve Wheeler
Plymouth
August 2020

Sequence

Six Letters

So you've picked up this book wondering what it's all about? Well, here to explain, is an open letter.

Uh … did I say open letter? It's actually six letters … do please read on.

This is my second book of poetry. I can't remember the day I first began to write poems, but it was a heck of a long time ago, definitely when I was still in primary school. I remember receiving a very high grade by submitting work that I had plagiarised (from a poem I found in a book) and passing it off as my own.

It was very wrong to do so, but the teacher was very dumb to believe that a seven year old boy could write poetry of such cadence, metre and profound meaning. Either that, or she simply wasn't paying attention (something *I* was accused of doing in school all the time). Teacher, teach thyself. All of the poems in this volume, I can assure you, are my own.

You will notice several strong themes running through this collection. One is relationships – predominantly relationships with a living God – the most powerful being in the universe – that everyone of us can enjoy if we know a simple truth.

Whether you believe in Him or not, it doesn't matter. You can still read these poems and think about your own relationships and what makes them succeed or fail. Poems work at several levels.

Another strong theme derives from the title of this book – Sacred. Look it up and you will discover that sacred signifies a connection with God. It also describes something or someone dedicated or set apart for His service or for His worship. That reflects my own faith in God and it emanates from just about everything I write. But the word sacred – and as a writer and poet I spotted this very quickly – is also a six letter word that can be manipulated into several anagrams. More on this in a moment.

Writing poetry, I have discovered, is similar to any other art. In song writing, you search for a memorable hook line and try to write lyrics that captivate or provoke. In painting the images are created not just to make you look, but to make you see.

I remember watching the movie *Dead Poets Society* in which the teacher (played by Robin Williams) tells his students to rip out the introduction to their poetry books – because it imposes dull rules that would ultimately stifle creativity. They do so with some trepidation, because they are not used to this kind of anarchy. But they do it anyway, and they are liberated because of this action.

My influences? *Dead Poets Society* is one of my favourite movies, because it celebrates the idea that there are no boundaries. I'll admit I have been influenced by poets such as Dylan Thomas, E.E. Cummings and Charles Bukowski, all of whom disregarded as many of the rules as they possibly could.

Rules in art are simply guidelines that can (and often should) be ignored if the artist wished to push the boat out and really make a statement. It's what happened in the time of the impressionists, the surrealists, the Pop artists, and also in movements such as Punk and New Wave. That's exactly what I aim to do with my poetry.

I don't always bother with scan and rhyme, although often it is there somewhere. I use words to craft an emotion, an image in the mind, or a vista of perception, and then the rules don't need to apply. And some of it may shock you, or make you uncomfortable. That's okay too.

For me, this is the literary equivalent of colouring outside the lines. I used to do that as a kid and was often reprimanded for it. But still I persisted, pushing the boundaries, stepping over the line. I have always loved to bend the rules and experiment.

So here's another experiment, one I have tried in this book. Throughout you'll see a few poems with titles comprising of the same six letters – look out, for example for Scared and Cedars. I hope you will have fun finding them and will appreciate them all.

Many of these poems are personal to me in some way – some are written abstractly and others relate to something that actually occurred in my life – Perfect Strangers is an example. Some were written way back in the 1980s and 90s. I just never got around to publishing them until now. Others were written more recently and reflect some of the current events currently in progress on the world stage.

I hope that every poem will evoke some meaning for you, even if you can't personally identify with them. I have written about the issues and challenges our world currently faces, especially poverty, toxic politics, pollution, climate change and racism. You will also see references to the 2020 virus pandemic, the Black Lives Matter movement and other world events of recent years.

You will also find that some of the poems have a reference to a scripture at the foot of the page. This is in case you feel the urge to delve deeper into the ideas and investigate further the motivation behind the writing of that poem particular poem.

My poems have been described as eclectic – they are written in a variety of styles, some in conventional metre and rhyme, others in a free verse style, and you will also find a few grime and hip hop lyrics too. I will admit that I often write in different styles depending on the mood I'm in but I also use them as a device to convey meaning and evoke emotions. Sometimes ideas and words flow more freely when you have a framework and sometimes it's better to be free of all constraints.

Back to experimentation I guess. Hopefully, combined, these features will paint a picture for you of my thoughts on our world, life, the universe and everything.

I really hope you enjoy reading these poems as much as I did writing them. And I hope you enjoy finding the six letters – or was it seven?

Steve Wheeler
Plymouth
August 2020

Honesty

Sitting alone
I feel the words
Paint pictures around my head
So I grab a few
And write them down upon
The page that holds
The story of my life

The thunder in the distance roars
As to the battle
In my mind
March the soldiers
Of my conscience
Intent on forcing me
To squeeze out
One more
Word of truth

Sacred Fire

I've walked on many lonely streets
I've knocked on many doors
I've shared my faith with gypsy kings
With Satanists and whores

I've found myself in places
I just didn't want to be
I've witnessed sights of hopelessness
I didn't want to see

I've flown too closely to the flame
I've balanced the high wire
But I'm wondering how much of this
Will burn up in the sacred fire
Yes I'm wondering how much of me
Will consume in the sacred fire

I've played on many stages
And I've sung so many songs
I've prayed for saints and sinners
And I've seen the rights and wrongs

I've travelled many weary miles
On many a foreign shore
I've spent my time in hotel rooms
And slept on bare board floors

I've plumbed the depths of deep despair
And I've soared on spiritual highs
But I'm wondering how much of this
Will burn up in the sacred fire
Yes I'm wondering how much of me
Will consume in the sacred Fire

1 Peter 1:6-7

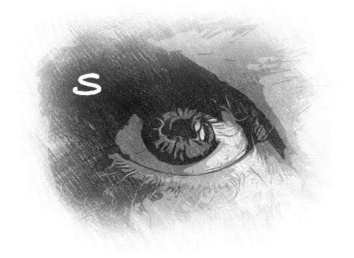

We are all lost souls together

We are all lost souls together,
each of us looking for a home
and I guess we all must wander
as we search for our Shalom.

In the dark we grope for exits
but it's the blind learning the blind
and we look in vain to find perfect peace
but when we do it's ill-defined
and we fail each time
and then we search for any
alternative solution we can find.

We try altering our consciousness
with opiates and wine,
but each and every time
we do we come crashing down
and we're worse off then
than when we first began.

Some look in dark places
and some change their faces,
while others sell their souls
and still others lose control.

We need a plan.
We need a helping hand.

We are all lost souls together
and my greatest fear for ever
is that humanity's time is running out
but not a single one of us
should be in any doubt
that there is someone
in a higher place
who has the power
to transcend time and space
and who intervened personally,
stepping into our history,
revealing to each of us the mystery
of how He can save humanity
from all of its iniquity
and can put our feet
upon a solid rock
to set us free.

He made the plan.
He is our helping hand.

We are all lost souls together
but if you think I'm gonna waste
my time arguing the toss,
you need to know that life isn't
negotiable and neither is the cross,
because it was the point in

—

space–time where He
suffered the greatest loss
to bring you and I to the point
where we are compelled to confess
that we have screwed it all up
and created this mess,
and nothing else in this world
or in the next
is gonna make it any less,
or change the fact that we are collectively
sending out a signal of distress.

He is the man,
and He is holding out
a helping hand.

Forgiveness

It's the best thing since sliced bread
It's the drink that went to your head
It's the thing that rights the wrong
It's that Mary Poppins song

It's that comfortable pair of shoes
It's the Mississippi delta blues
It's the cream before the jam
It's the wham bam thank you ma'am

It's your favourite album track
It's the nothing that you lack
It's getting a good night's sleep
It's that photo you secrete

It's your favourite movie star
You met randomly in a bar
It's a sunny autumn sky
And the answer to your every why

It's a playful puppy dog
It's living high upon the hog
It's your treasured memories
It's the buzzing of the bees

It's your garden in the sun
It's a second Belgian bun
It's a holiday for two in Spain
It's holding hands in the pouring rain

But the best life you will ever live
is when two wounded hearts forgive

No Surprise

He hangs
He dies
You live
Your lies
He speaks
The truth
You ask
For proof
He bleeds
He cries
You compromise
He knocks
Your door
And you ignore
He pays
The price
You throw
The dice
No surprise …
Snake eyes

Sacred

And still they ran toward that barren hill
While skies grew dark to split the air with fire
And gathered there to watch the dreadful kill
Before the rains fell turning earth to mire

Then darkness fell to form a silent shroud
Befitting for a stark brutality profound
As silence hushed the hillside like a cloud
The tortured man gave forth one final sound

The man abandoned there to die alone
His battered body broken and abused
Had bowed his will before his Father's throne
To pray for those who tortured and accused

This final sacrificial act before he died
Revealed his truth to those

who gazed upon his face
Showing each the purpose that it signified
The redemption of the entire human race

This act of dark and bleak insanity
Carried out upon that Palestinian incline
Had been preordained
        to purchase all humanity
The culmination of God's ultimate design

Romans 8:1

Perfect Strangers

I ain't gonna lie 'cos I'm afraid you won't believe this, that you'll find this next story so incredible that you might not receive this but I'm gonna tell it anyway because this really happened to me and I've got nothing to lose I'm a tell it faithfully; this is not something you can put down to a false memory.

When life throws you serious shade and you find yourself in danger the very last thing you expect is to get assistance from a perfect stranger but that's exactly what happened to my parents and I when I was only twelve years old and I thought we were all going to die but we were miraculously saved by the intervention of two passers-by.

We were trying to drive home on a deserted icy road and that night as the snow blew in it was treacherous and cold and we came a bit too quickly around a bend in the road and my Dad lost control and the next thing we knew we were heading toward the edge of a cliff and the only thing that stopped us was a rock sticking out of a huge snow drift.

Our car stopped dead at a peculiar inclination and in the dark we saw through the windows that we were in a dangerous condition. My Dad couldn't reverse the car because the back wheels were off the ground and all we could hear was the axel spinning hopelessly round and round and the snow kept falling as the temperature dropped down and down.

Then from outside the car I saw two figures approaching together but there shouldn't have been anyone outside in that appalling weather but there they were standing outside the car and with my Dad they started conversing and told him to get back in the car and get those gears reversing and then they lifted the car back onto its wheels like it was some kind of plaything.

We were all very grateful for the help of two perfect strangers who had definitely saved our lives from that imminent danger so my Dad got out to thank them but he could see nobody there, the place where they had been standing was now totally bare because they had apparently disappeared without a trace into thin air.

Now you can explain this any way you like or dismiss it as a hoax but I'm telling you that being stranded in a car in a blizzard is no joke.

But God says he will never leave us nor forsake us and that He'll send his angels to rescue us so the rocks and stones are unable to break us and that's exactly what I believe happened that night when those two men came to save us.

He sent two perfect strangers so the blizzard wouldn't take us.

Hebrews 13:2

Key

In the dungeons of his keep
He locked me up
And threw away the key

Then you risked
Your life and limb
And climbed down
To where I was
In the darkness
Of that cell

You made a key
Out of your heart
To unlock the door
And laid down your life
As the bridge
For my escape

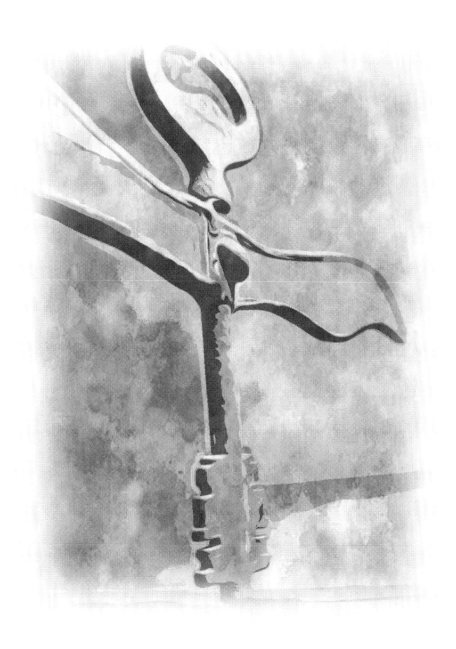

Blood Transfusion

You were like a hypodermic –
an injection that went
straight to my head

I got you under my skin
but you turned sceptic

It took a very special doctor
to diagnose my condition

It took a courageous operation
to prevent me from
developing of septicaemia

It took a dedicated man
to die
during the process

Ephesians 1:7

Urban Transgression

1: Serious Games

Serious games that people play as they make their
way across their day //

Put it down on record put it down to experience
just put it down //
We're all living in this world
living in the real world surviving in
a cruel world
this is no rehearsal
for a play // electric world
eclectic world
digital daze plastic haze
oh my days // destructive world
seductive world head in a whirl
is it a boy or a girl?
Fast moving inner grooving

nothing soothing disapproving
earthmoving everything pays
everyone knows
everything goes
everything shows
and everyone goes

Serious games that people play as they make their
way across their day //

.   Found your way out yet solved the riddle?
Everybody realises that it'll be worse
when you're caught in the middle of
a busy five lane highway you shouldn't be there
horns blare you should be somewhere //
disappearing down the back streets
and dirty cul-de-sacs run down council flats plastic
bags and the detritus on the stair // concrete and
glass reflect you as you pass
none of this is gonna last // lost in
the concrete jungle vertical monoliths
virginal skies dry your eyes don't sympathise
no-one believes you
and your sophisticated lies

Serious games that people play as they make their
way across their day //

Up and down the stairwells, elevator broken yet
again and there is no lift to the weather
grey and ashen overhead

---

and overheads are crippling in this
one man business down town and
down and out lost in the crowd
say it out loud you need to stay proud
no funeral shroud // the audience looks on
anticipating and the word is oscillating
as if they think they're participating
in the human race // but the hopes dissipate
and no-one is willing to pay the going rate
while the electorate vacillates
and the violence in the cities escalates
and pollution levels raise the stakes
until the prophets cry out "it's too late!"

Serious games that people play as they make their
way across the day //

Back street shot gun fires life is a pump action
life is a reaction // "Hey get a load of that"
street life right between the eyes
and it's no surprise //
the inner city violence of the urban terror boys
you can watch in horror as the mob deploys
and it comes to the surface
and attempts to systematically destroy
everything that is already damaged
beyond repair but it's all hot air
in a city of despair

and the serious games that people play as they make
their way across their day //

———

Hell, it's an all-out war it's a war
we're in trying to survive by the colour of our skin
and the skin of our teeth
and you're either downed underneath
by a cop with a knee on your neck
or furred up arteries and a heart attack
// life is a pump action life is a reaction
and I gasp for breath // see that? girl,
you look // no stockings short skirt heels
ankle bracelet no time for you no time for me
rushing headlong to her destiny
raped in an alley way
two hours after you read this...

Serious games that people play as they make their
way across the day //

Whose fault is all this and who wants to know?
Hell, what do any of us really know
about living and being a being
a human being and are we looking
without seeing // interfacing with
the concrete and steel of a
neighbourhood that is beginning to reel
from the nightmare deal
of the serious games we are playing
I'm just saying //
as the paramedics are felled
by mindless actions
of the immoral ones

and the body count rises
and the country subsides in a reckless tide
of homicides and suicides
and taking sides and the very fabric of
our democracy dies //

How the hell can I be expected
to raise a child in this kind of world?
Where is the hope for our nation,
for this generation?

Serious games that people play as they make their
way across their day //

2: Hide your ears and eyes

I dread it when the sun goes down
I dread it when the news comes on

You can laugh at the newspapers

The sensationalist red tops
with their hyperbole
and the hearsay
the profit making
rabble quenching
front-paging
centre-
staging
ever-raging
fist clenching
issue selling
gut wrenching
editorials you can
take it or leave it

But you can't argue
with full motion technicolour
TV images of misery

\\

It's the real thing
We dare you to take
the challenge
Take just one sip
We think
you will
agree

\\

Closing captions
Signature tune

<   Fade to grey   >

3: Ask them

Stop the old lady
    who wears the golden crown
Stop her and ask her
    and also the injured policeman
    laying on the ground
Ask him too

Ask the window cleaner
    and the stock market dealer
Ask the ice cream man
    and the guy from Turkmenistan
Ask the destitute sleeping wino
    and the Berlin zookeeper with his rhino

Ask the girl outside the casino
    and the Italian bambino
    and the entire population of Reno
    and the state of San Marino

Ask the midwife doing her rounds
    and the aristocrat in his grounds
Ask the owner of the stray dog
    and the woman out for her morning jog

Ask the social worker
Ask the council leader

Ask the Asian shop keeper
        and the part-time road sweeper
Ask the old man coughing on the park bench
And the oil-stained mechanic holding the wrench
        and the pop star riding high at number one
        and the DJ
        and the man who was burnt in the sun

Ask the exhausted on-call medic
Ask the aesthetic and the eccentric
Ask the sinner, ask the saint
Ask the man whose clothing is covered in paint
Ask the star studded case of a West End musical
And the gamblers who throw their dice
        and lose it all

Ask the Prime Minister
        and the Leader of the Opposition
Ask those who are opposed to both those positions
Ask Mohammed, Christ and Buddha
Ask your father and your mother
Ask your sister and your brother
        and those no longer speaking to each other

Ask the captain of a nuclear submarine
Ask the artist who only paints in shades of green
Ask the man who always
        shouts out something obscene

———

As those who are heard but never seen

Ask the Senior citizens and their spouses
        and all the residents of London's penthouses
Ask the CBI executive and his secret lover
        and those who are neither
        one thing or the other

Ask the one year old baby in the pram
        and just about every American
Ask the people of Europe and the Westminster peers
Ask the cynics and critics who do nothing but sneer
Ask the bus driver
        and the man with the wax in his ears
Ask the young girl who's sat there in floods of tears

Ask the blind ones and those using walking frames
And all those you have met
        but can't recall their names
Ask the wild hearted artists whom nobody tames
        and the boys in their bedrooms
        playing video games

Ask the exhausted young nurses
        and those without hope
And the paranoid people who've run out of soap
Ask the Archbishop of Canterbury
        and also the Pope
And the millions of users addicted to dope
And the postal workers and the cleaners
And the underhand schemers

—

And the romantic dreamers

Ask the mathematicians who are calculating
Ask the customer held for an hour on call waiting
    and the man who is late
        and who just lost his car keys down the grating

Ask the teenage girl who has just started dating
        and the crowds who are standing and waiting
        and the military commanders
        their fingers hesitating

Ask them

Ask them all

And they will all tell you
This is too great a price
For anyone to pay.

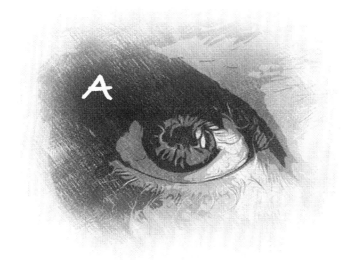

Vertical Ellipsis

Life was a tedious vacuum, void
empty as a lockdown parking lot and so devoid
of any moral compass or self-sacrifice
and so I fell the victim of my own device

Vacant conscience made unruly space
for every misdemeanour lacking grace
to come and dwell within my fractured mind
a base and soulless great divide defined

Intentional omission of the holy fire
No loss of meaning within my own desire
a vertical ellipsis made by stubborn will
secreted deep inside a spirit running still

And in this way hubris and arrogance
became the tunes to call my tortured dance
The tempo brought me to my broken knees
where finally heaven bent to hear my pleas

By falling short I reaped the storm I'd sown
but wished that vertical ellipsis overthrown
Then to me came the Nazarene
transformed my raiment pure and clean

I know that my redemption will not fail
my debts paid in their fullness on the nail
Firm foundations based on perfect love
my eyes now firmly fixed on that above

Deep Clean

I have a vacuum cleaner
That cleans the carpet well
It deals with all the messy stains
And takes away the smell
It picks up toe nail clippings
And a hundred kinds of bits
It gathers up the ear wax
And incarcerates the nits

It eradicates the fluff and stuff
And every kind of dander
It cleans up every surface
From the backdoor to the front door
It clears out nooks and crannies
And scours every niche
It sucks up cake and biscuit crumbs
And dried up bits of quiche

What annoys me most of all
Is the cleaning never ends
No matter how you suck it up
The more the dust descends
And when its little bag is full
It's emptied in the bin
And then the cycle starts again -

It's a lot like me, and sin

I have a vacuum cleaner
That cleans my carpet well
It deals with the unsavoury
But it can't save me from Hell
My soul was deeply stained by sin
Through wilful dark manoeuvres
Then Jesus Christ deep cleaned my soul
Much better than a hundred Hoovers

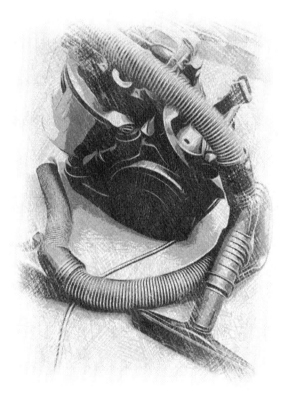

Isaiah 64:6

Scared

To be honest I ain't afraid of much in this life and there ain't many things that can bring me a sense of strife but there's one thing that unnerves me so much it cuts me like a knife and it still frightens me and sends my imagination into overdrive and I worry that it's something I maybe won't survive and nobody, not any of us, will be
coming out of this alive.

I ain't gonna lie when I tell you that out of all the events in my life I've been through just about the only thing that has ever torn me in two is knowing that I've done and said things that have hurt or damaged you. And if you were anything like me, you might not be willing to forget but in the process of redemption I know you have never ever yet held anything against me and although I still bitterly regret all the things I've done,
you never fail to write off my debt.

I know you said no-one could ever pluck me from your hand, but I'm still running scared and I don't yet fully understand how I could properly find

security and feel safe in your hands but it still
worries me that all those daily demands on my time
and my occasional rebellion might countermand any
benefits I've gathered as I've tried to serve faithfully
at your command.

So I find myself running constantly from any worldly
distraction, and I have a lot of angst about missing
out on the action and I spend much of my time trying
to avoid the opposing faction. The greatest fear I
have is falling away and losing my passion for
serving you and living a life that fails
to acknowledge your compassion.
So I'm a grab hold of your forgiveness
like it's going out of fashion.

Words

Words are a weapon, words are a sword
Words can be a punishment or a reward
Words can be empty devoid of meaning
Words can be uplifting or demeaning

Words can hurt or words can heal
Words are an accelerator fuel
to burn with intensity and with fire
or land you on a funeral pyre

Words may comfort, words may challenge
Stabilise with kindness or unbalance
Words can be a garden that grows
With unwanted weeds or a beautiful rose

Words can be used for harm or for good
Words are like nails hammered into wood
You can take them back and try to be kind
But there's always a nail hole left behind

James 3: 5-9

These people are losers

Jeb Bush is a low energy stiff

Rosie O'Donnell's disgusting, both inside and out

Carly Fiorina is terrible at business

Sacha Baron Cohen is a moron

Jon Stewart is a joke, not very bright and totally over[?]

Cher is somewhat of a loser

Lord Sugar – you're a total loser who Piers Morgan do[?]

[?]ink is very smart or very rich

[?] people are losers

[?] the real Lord that Donald Trump exists

Never Enough

There's not enough gold
    in the world's bank reserves
To buy the security
    you think you will need
You'll be searching in vain
    for the joy you deserve
In the stories you hear
    or the books that you read

There's no value in any
    of the movies you view
That can bring you the wisdom
    you desperately crave
There ain't enough good
    in the good works you do
To guarantee that your eternal
    soul will be saved

You can listen to music
    'till you're deaf in both ears
But the tunes and the lyrics
    will fail to inspire
They will never assuage
    all your deep seated fears

Nor will they satisfy
	your deepest desire

You can familiarise yourself
	with the finest of wines
But the bottle will not
	define your happiness
Pharma and meds in all
	their sophisticated designs
Will only contribute further
	to your helplessness

You can look for thrills all over
	and seek them randomly
But if you need a solution
	I will give just the one
I tell you it now and
	I tell you in all honesty
To escape from your darkness
	you must follow the Son

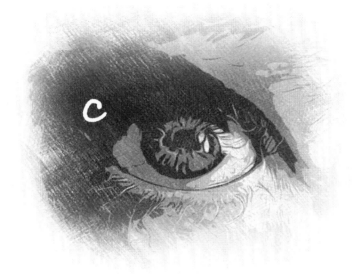

I Seek No Reward

I seek no earthly reward
on my shoulder no sword
I want none of the trappings
nor medals or wrappings
This is not what I'm working toward

No ribbons on my breast
and no trophies in my chest
No congratulatory diplomas
and no heady aromas
to signify any brief earthly success

I want no honorary plaque
nor even a pat on the back
But it will be music to my ears
when finally I hear:
"Well done, faithful servant,
enter My Kingdom here."

Luke 6:23

Red S.A.C.

Red is not a colour we usually associate with peace nor is it very evocative of visions of release // more likely red is used to stop a speeding driver in his tracks or given as a sign of danger of impending attacks but here are the facts // believe me when I tell you that in an eternal context, red is the colour that aptly represents a solution to the many problems humanity must face and is a revolution that will change the destiny of the entire human race

Now that may sound like an unbelievable claim but please have patience and give me a chance explain // red is the colour of blood and if I can be more candid // it is also the colour of redemption and a response to the evil that man did when he rebelled at the very beginning in the garden // and his mind turned away from his creator as his disobedience began to harden

The ancient texts say that without the shedding of blood there can be no atonement for sins and no covering for the things that have separated us from God // the problem is sin separates and divides and there's nothing we can do // no good works or words we can provide that will make us a bridge back to God across the great divide // so it's obvious the solution had to come from His side.

And that's what He did he made a provision for us when He sent His Son Jesus to die on a cross // red is the one thing that can defeat the enemy of our souls and it's the only substance on Earth that can really make us whole // red is the colour of the blood that was spilt at Calvary to give us a bridge back to God that was built on His sacrifice and can save us no matter what we've done in our lives

Here's the deal, and it's not complicated and I'm not making this up because in the Bible it is stated that if you tell God you're sorry for the thing you've said and done // all the stuff that you're ashamed of and wish you'd not begun and all the many webs of lies that you've deliberately spun // then God says you're a part of His family if you accept that His one and only Son Jesus died in your place // and that He took the hit for you through his love and in his grace

So let me lay out for you the bottom line // we can do absolutely nothing to earn God's favour // in fact we all deserve eternal punishment for the fruits of our labour // for not loving God with all our hearts while we're dissing our neighbours // and the only way we'll ever make it is with the help of a saviour

The only thing that has the power to wash any of us clean is the blood of the Lamb that was spilt in the closing scene on the cross on that God forsaken Judean hillside // where Jesus laid aside any human pride // and put any proud ambitions to one side and said "Forgive them Father" as he bled out and died

Red S.A.C. is a title that needs some explanation and this might be the most important exposition you're ever gonna get your hands on // it's something that everyone can understand and it's better than any wisdom man says // if they only knew the truth and can see all of this through God's lenses // the blood of Christ is all we need //Red Saves And Cleanses

1 John 1:7

Mountains

I am told
That without love
I am as a sounding brass
But without you
There is no brass
To sound upon

I am told
That if I move mountains
And have no love
I am nothing

But the mountain of your love
Has moved me

And I am something

Low Voltage Prayer

I
talk
to You

You
talk
to me

We
talk
to each other

How come sometimes
You can't hear me
because my line is so bad

and I can't hear you
because my actions
speak louder
than your words?

Double Agent

I'm an assassin of truth; I'm a double agent
I hide in the shadows, as my lies I invent
I play two opposing roles that contradict
My double dealing leads me into conflict

My identity is fluid; I work undercover
I rapidly switch between traitor and lover
adopting many strange and incompatible positions
unable to reconcile contrasting propositions

I know what's right, and know what I should do
but like a moth to the flame, I'm attracted to
a dangerous and destructive fiery light
and I find myself choosing wrong instead of right

I'm constant but capricious
trusting yet suspicious
I'm truthful but mendacious
staid and yet outrageous
I'm thoughtful but unfeeling
hidden yet revealing

I wound instead of healing
I'm standing when I'm kneeling

I live a double life both awake
and in my dreams
What you think you see of me
is not what it seems

Beneath this cool surface
I'm a mine of contradictions
Don't be too surprised
when I confound your predictions

You can tell me by the ways
my mind is always changing
An identity crisis that
is constantly rearranging

I've build my foundations
on shifting sands
with my two faced double standards
and the blood on my hands

Romans 3:2

Discovery

I spent two years at art school
where I learnt to search
the depths inside my soul
that could be so finitely expressed
by separating such diverse parts from the
whole.

I practiced my guitar by night
and crafted songs with words and tunes
and thus through playing out
the rhythm of my life
I discovered hidden words within the runes.

And there I learnt a vital truth
as wisdom fell across my pathway like a tree
where through me coursed the deepest grace
like a flood through each
and every part of me.

Romans 6:14

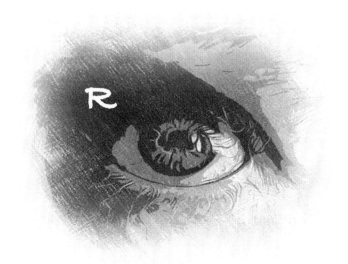

Agapē Love

Your love is invisible but it shows
Your love is organic and it grows
Your love is resilient and remains
Your love is everlasting and sustains

Your love is so remarkable it amazes
Your love is so stunning that it dazes
Your love is unexpected and it surprises
Your love is arresting and it hypnotises

Your love is undeserving and it shames
Your love is individual and it names
Your love is esoteric and it mystifies
Your love is so shocking it electrifies

Your love is outrageous it terrifies
Your love is purity and it justifies
Your love is so fulfilling it satisfies
Your love is unending it never dies

Your love is uplifting and it elevates
Your love is inspiring and it motivates
Your love is so strong that it prevails
Your love is so reliable it never fails

 Nought

Every morning you wake
All the love you can fake
All the hearts that you break
All the pain you can take
Every ache you can ache
Every noise you can make
All the mud you can rake
Every wager you stake

Every game that you play
All the insults you say
All the fears kept at bay
Every due that you pay
Every time that you stray
Every hour in each day
All the prayers that you pray
Every time you delay

All the lies you can spin
Every battle you win
All the smiles you can grin
Every sin you can sin
Every mile you can walk
All the victims you stalk
All the words you can talk

Every blackboard you chalk

Every user you troll
All the votes you can poll
Every item you stole
And the dice that you roll
All the wages you earn
And the bridges you burn
All the heads that you turn
And the lessons you learn

Every place you can go
And the things you can know
All the chances you blow
All the tantrums you throw
Every time you say no
All the seeds that you sow
In the sun and the snow
As above so below

Each assignment you grade
Every meal you have made
All the deals you can trade
All the debts you have paid
Every role you have played
All your knowledge conveyed

As below so above
They are nought
Without love

1 Cor 13:2

Heart of Ice

My sin
My pride

His hands
His side

My fear
My dread

His feet
His head

My deepest stain
His grief
His pain

My heart of ice
His sacrifice

Party Games

They'll talk about taxes
and they'll argue the toss
They'll debate the economy
profits and loss
They'll shout about Brexit
and foreign exchange
and bang on the table
like someone deranged

Employment and health
are the issues they crave
and in spite of the optics
they still misbehave
The sleaze and the greed
are the current events
but ask a straight question
and they'll sit on the fence

They shout in the House
'til they're blue in the face
with freedom of speech
and a swing of the mace

They talk about anything

'worthy of note'
that's been carefully tabled
with one eye on the vote

But ask them of Jesus
and what He has said
or quiz them on where
they'll end up when they're dead
Try to discover
if they're lost or they're saved
and if they believe
that He rose from the grave

and they go strangely silent
with nothing to say

but although
there is no comment

it won't go away

Cadres

Noisy shouters,
Down and outers
Conspiracy theorists
Spreading fearists

Science doubters
Rule flouters
What abouters
Lager louters

Toothless cryers
Truthless liars
Snake oil buyers
Climate change deniers

Trolling sneerers
Haters, jeerers
Profiteerers
Selective hearers

News presenters
Crooked mentors
Life preventers
Confidence denters

Politicians
Statisticians
Bad musicians
Meteorological conditions

Hands Up

Hands up
all those
who love me

Put your hands in the air
if you really care

Hands up
if you're prepared
to take the blame
for all my wrongdoing

Hold your hands up high

Lift them high
and keep them there
for about
two thousand years

Luke 23:33

Eyes

Darkness was his
　　a pool of blackness his abode

But then he cried out
　　in his bitterness
　　and was met with hands
　　that touched and gave light
　　that brought sweetness
　　that lifted a heavy load

Blind eyes can see
　　but those with sight
　　may choose between
　　what they wish to see

And that which
　　they would rather
　　disregard

John 9 (the entire chapter)

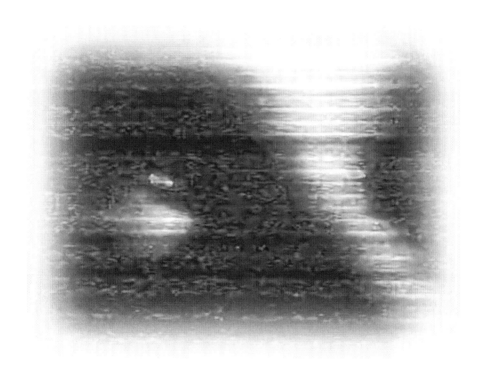

Innocent

Yeah, He died a criminal's death
Even though He was innocent to His final breath
They hung Him up between the earth and the sky
And He carried our sins
     and our debts and our failures and our lies.
It wasn't the iron nails that held Him there
It was His love for you and me
     that fixed him on the tree
Yeah, he was the sacrificial lamb
Who spilt His blood, the great I Am
He was the bridge between humanity
     and the Creator
The incarnation of love, He was not a hater.
And as His blood flowed down
     and drenched the soil below
He said forgive them 'cos they really do not know
What they're doing and they act as though
     they are blind
To the truth that I am doing this for all mankind.

But it won't even make a difference to you
Unless you decide his promises were true
And that He was who He said He was
And that He died in your place on the cross.

—

Listen - what you're hearing is not a fairy story
And I'm not telling you this just to get some glory.
He gave up His life for you, and I'm not gonna lie
When I say that if you don't even try
To understand the magnitude of what He's done
That He's not only real,
        but He's also the promised One,
You gonna miss out on everything
        He's got planned for you
And that's still much more than you're entitled to.

Yeah He was innocent
And it was His sole intent
To buy us all back from the malcontent
To redeem us, 'cos that was exactly why He was sent.
That if it wasn't for all the blood He spilt
You and I would still be standing in our guilt
To save you and me from Hell
        and outer darkness and to prevent
Us from deviating from the way that was meant.
And this is not some story that the weak invent
To be a crutch for them when they cannot be content
With their lives and the trouble
        they get themselves in.
No, the bloody execution on that hill
        was a real event.

Yeah He was innocent
But the authorities managed to invent
A lot of lies and fake news that sealed his fate
And they sent Him to an early grave in their hate.

But it wasn't for long 'cos three days later
He was seen alive and
        walking in the neighbourhood.
'Cos He conquered death
        just like He said He would
And even if you don't believe this is true
And if you deny it with everything you do
And everyone who's in your crew
Uses His name like it's nothing new
Or some cuss word to throw around
Just because they like the way that it sound
He still gonna hold his hand out to you
And call your name like He always will do
Cos He'll never give up on you
No He'll never stop from
        calling out to you
He'll never turn His back on you
He'll leave the ninety-nine
        to come find you
No He'll never give up on anyone,
No not even you.

He was innocent

1 Peter 1:19

Human Condition

I eat what I want to eat
Drink what I want to drink
Say what I want to say
Think what I want to think.
I read what I want to read
See what I want to see
Act like I want to act
Be who I want to be.

I stop when I want to stop
Say what I want to say
Fight like I want to fight
Play how I want to play.
I go where I want to go
Leave when I want to leave
Hide what I want to hide
Believe what I want to believe.

I love who I want to love
Cry when I want to cry
Laugh when I want to laugh
Lie like I always lie.
I sin like I want to sin
Choose who I want to choose
Ignore who I want to ignore
I will lose like I always lose

Isaiah 53:6

Oh, the Irony!

John Lennon sang
"Happiness is a Warm Gun"
then an assassin shot him dead
thus cutting off any more pearls of wisdom
What's left unsaid will remain unsaid

George Washington
had much political bite
and fought long for freedom from tyranny
His teeth were taken from the slaves he owned
so his entire life was contradictory

And, irony of ironies –
the greatest irony of them all:
man was told he would become like a god
and that was just before his fall

Success & Failure

Success comes in a can
Failure comes in a can't
Warnings come in a don't
Rebellion comes in a shan't

Guilt comes in a shouldn't
Reluctance comes in a wouldn't
Regrets come in a didn't
Fear comes in a couldn't

Bad News Sells

You roll the press broadcast the news but it's only propaganda to you because all you care about is another million views // and everything that others do you criticise and you say few of their actions are sound or wise and unless any of it jives or coincides with your political agenda successes are ignored and left unrecognised // you take delight in pointing out the flaws in new ideas so that innovation flees whenever you appear // you and your media buddies do not seem to be at all concerned that the mental health of people can crash and burn if you persist in feeding us only the problems you have discerned.

There's not a single thing that can be done or said that doesn't rankle in your head or end up on your cutting room floor you're continually digging dirt on the how-to and what-for // you target the rich and famous and ignore the poor outside your door and you're highlighting the flaws and warning us all there's worse to come but you know for sure // sensationalist headlines sell so you persist in spewing out your particular form of journalistic hell because as everybody knows the darker the news is the more it will sell.

Picking faults cannot be a feat that's pulled off easily nor is it easy to defeat // when you are constantly on our screens and in our face and it cannot be a happy place for you to be // when you are stuck in the mode of dissing constantly what other people see as a useful solution or dismissing a remedy but instead you're on your website riffing constantly // about what's wrong or dangerous or how things will get worse instead of better it's almost like you're waging some kind of vendetta // and you're raking up the dirt on every trend setter as you travel round world like a sordid jet setter and you wonder why we all think you live in the gutter?

If only you were more constructive in your constant criticism and used your investigative skills to apply an alternative prism or attempted to employ some entertaining witticism to lighten the mood of your gloomy pessimism but no // you drag us down your road of nihilism denying any hope to those who need a dose of optimism it's as though we're all living inside a prison being forced to stare at your televised narcissism.

It's a crying shame you have so much influence and reach and yet you choose to instruct and teach us all to see the mud instead of the stars and you bend the truth to bolster who you are and focus solely on the ratings war // you have the weirdest compulsion to grab and pinch the very essence of hope away from us like some grasping grinch because the only thing you are more intent on selling is another column inch.

So while you're standing there telling us why it can't be done there are those out there who are working quietly like one to accomplish the very thing you said was impossible to get done // but that matters little to you even though they made it possible because the next thing is you point out a dozen reasons why it's improbable and you try to make every solution some kind of obstacle // what you and the other hacks are doing is contemptible but here's another story you won't find acceptable // if everyone stopped reading your news your poison would be preventable.

Front Page News

They didn't bother
to put the news of the execution
on the front page

It wasn't even a page two story –
murderers and criminals
were put to death every day
and today appeared to be
no exception

Blame it on the Romans
they might be right
they might be wrong
Leave it to the obituaries

The newspaper man
moves through the crowd
while his thoughts
move through his mind

What if the man was innocent?
What had that to do with him?

They said he healed the sick

Opened blind eyes
Even raised the dead!

Well, now he's dead too.
Let's see if he can
raise himself up!

Someone said he was a king
but that just had to be rumours

You see
if he was a king of this world
he would have stood and fought
he would have called his army in

There would have been a massacre!

Now *that* would have been
front page news!

The newspaper man
trudges slowly down the street
totally unaware
that in less than three days
he will be announcing

The greatest story
of all time ...

John 11:25-26

Vanishing Point

In the heat of the fighting
when the battle seemed lost,
And the men were soul weary,
despairing the cost,
From the ranks a solitary figure broke
And through the smoke
He crossed the divide
And on both sides
Two companies of soldiers
stopped and stared.

He wielded no weapon
but stretched out his arms
As though a surrender was offered
Vulnerable then, and open to fire
He pressed steadily forward
across the ravaged ground.
The enemy horde fixed their gazed on him
And although the opportunity to kill presented itself,
not a shot was sent
As boldly he negotiated
the quagmire and remnants
Of once living creatures and men.

Then came he to a point
in the midst of the silent havoc
Which now was quiet and calm in the gloom
And he halted and looked at the ground,
bent himself down
And then held up
a solitary bloom.

This flash of colour
in the backdrop of grey and dun
Evoked a contrast that shone
as brightly as the noonday sun
And the brief respite of peace that it brought
Within a black day of eruptions
and death and destruction
Gave two entire battalions pause for thought
And made them ponder
what was the cause
For which they so valiantly fought?

For there in No-Man's land,
in nineteen hundred and seventeen
A saviour like a vision,
just as suddenly as he had appeared
Now as quickly
Like a vapour,
Disappeared

Power is Transitory

I'm not a glory seeker but I am a fighter. I've never been a novelist but I am a writer, and in all my days and in all my ways I've tried to be a straight-sighter firing my literary bullets into the dark to try to make it lighter.

I'm a lyricist and whether in a poem or in prose I'm a line-by-line pugilist and while the opposition runs and hides I slug it out to document the ugliness of society's great divides.

I'm a partisan and my conscience tells me I'm a take sides, because injustice is everywhere and whatever the state provides will never be enough to heal humanity's wounded insides and there's never gonna be any place to hide because injustice and deprivation always coincide.

Successive governments rise and grab it all and then they lose their popularity, meet their demise and fall, and they'll promise you just about anything to persuade you to heed their political call but if they think that's how the story ends they're heading for an even bigger fall.

Because the power of the politician is transitory, and nothing really changes.

No it's something we can't ignore, you see society is still rotten through to the core where the rich get richer while the poor stay poor and politicians should always be judged on whether they've made any difference at all.

Politicians come to power and they look for fame, but how many of us can remember any of their names, 'cos the bottom line is no sooner than they screw it up they resign and someone else has to take the blame and they do their continuous damage and none of them show any shame.

It's a constant rearrangement and it's played out like it was a board game.

No one who ever expresses the remotest desire to seize a position of power should ever be allowed to acquire authority over the people 'cos when it goes down to the wire they show no remorse as they pursue their ideological desire and none of them is willing to pull us out from the fire.

The power we gain in the here and now is transitory, it passes in a flash and that goes with the territory because no matter how we try to hold on to our personal glory it slips right through our grasping fingers with alacrity and the next thing we know we're standing right there in eternity and it's only then that we discover with a stone cold certainty that His is the only real kingdom and power and permanent glory.

And that's the real story.

Power is transitory.

Matthew 6:13

Pray Hard

Pray hard so you don't fall into temptation
So you have no hesitation
So there is no complication
Pray hard in the day and in the night,
and in all points in between
Pray so that in your doubt
you hold a truth that is unseen

Pray hard in all things,
and in all things give your praise
So that in all things you know
there is reason for your days
Pray hard today and pray hard tomorrow
Pray so that joy will stave off all your sorrow

Pray in the good things and also in the bad
Pray hard and constantly,
in all the hours to be had
Pray even though you feel
as though your prayers may not be known
Pray hard, because through all of this,
your prayers will reach His throne

1 Thessalonians 5:17

Falling Structures

Inside the urban labyrinth
I came across an empty plinth
A place once occupied, that now
was empty, and I wondered how
a statue of such strong construction
could suffer great humiliation.

How what was once so safe and sound
could end up crashing to the ground,
its fractured pieces scattered far
and wide across the blackened tar.

The symbol of a darker time
was lying in the road supine,
no longer able to demand
attention, reverence or command.

And then a voice spoke in my ear
"This statue represented fear;
of bondage and a great oppression."

So I asked, in deep depression,
why would such structures be erected
so evil could be so prominently represented?

The answer came as I looked down
and saw the shoe marks all around,
that were not black, nor brown, nor white
but neutral prints, and then I saw the light:

When hatred speaks and you and I
ignore the threat and turn blind eyes,
symbols of hate and oppression thrive
to become the strong structures
that dominate our lives.

John 15:21

Dawn

The sun hangs high suspended now
Like hawk about to strike his foe
This sphere of power
Has in its hour
Of glory in creation's power
Brushed night and darkness low
Gone now the painted jewels
On heaven's brow

Creative

Set the thoughts in fluid motion
Motivate the literary urge
Capture every fleeting notion
Feed that wild creative surge

Flutter like a little child
Fill the canvas using fingers
Mix the flowing pigments wild
Catch the fragrance as it lingers

Forge the bonds between the lines
Make the notes flow crossing borders
Create the ambience of the mind
Loose every element of order

Gratitude

When it comes to being honest
I can celebrate the fact
That in all my years on this good earth
There is nothing I have lacked

And yet in other countries
People far less fortunate than I
Are forced to live in squalor
Some are sick and often die

When it comes to being grateful
I can hold my hand on heart
And hope in others' suffering
I may never play a part

Trans/ /mission

1: CD Ears

From the start the Word was uttered into a void
of dark dimensions \ an anechoic chamber that
absorbed its strong vibrations \ but still some
heard the cadence even though it was dispersed \
and responded to its message to escape the
human curse \\

The Word was a love letter sent to the entire
human race \ and here's a mystery the Word was
God but showed a human face \ to you and me
and walked around pure spirit made in flesh \ a
stupendous divine presence although some
would not be impressed \\

Most failed to spot the message deep embedded
in its lode \ even though the signal boosted
power from clear to overload \ they chose to
ignore the message and its promises untold \ and
deleted it because they failed to read the object
code \\

Now our ears are captured by CDs and
downloads that appeal \ and the sounds
surround and immerse us and give us all the feels
\ yet the Word still speaks and beckons us to hear
the truth revealed \ but few have time to listen
and fewer still are healed \\

from the condition that afflicts us all despite our
hopes or fears \ and while we're slowly passing
through this temporal veil of tears \ we assume
that this is all there is that no more is to come \
but the Word persists and whispers through the
cosmic background hum \\

And still the Word reverberates down through our history \ and still today we can each gain access to the mystery \ of how the Word became flesh to walk and live among us \ all we need do is open up the Book and listen to the chorus \ of the good news incarnate that calms our minds and fears \ transmitted from the heart of the Creator into our CD ears \\

2: Signal Strength

I tune into your frequency when I'm within your range and reach / by ramping up my volume to detect the subtle nuance of your speech / my headphones boost the signal and you're inside my head with me / instead of being distant separated by the gulf of eternity //

When I tune in to your broadcast your words delve deep within / but my reception often dips through interference caused by sin / so I focus more intently and I listen hard and long / but it's difficult to tether so our contact is prolonged //

There's a cross compatibility when our frequencies collide / and a mutual exchange affirms the nexus of both sides / my trust in your great faithfulness becomes my personal Bluetooth / while your propagation beacon clearly transmits your Word of truth //

The signal to noise ratio is quite often off the scale / but I know that with persistence I will very rarely fail / because I can trust that your clear transmission will maintain hi fidelity / and I know that through it all your signal strength will save and rescue me //

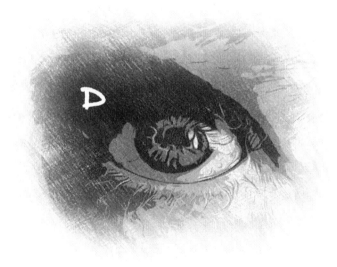

Destiny

What is your destiny?
What are you meant to be?
What future do you see?
What is your destiny?

What happens when we die isn't something we think about while we're in our prime / it's something we prefer to defer in favour of the present time / but the future of our lives is something we are all connected with / and whether you die early or whether you have a lot longer left to live / it's a stone cold certainty that every one of us eventually dies / but before death knocks upon your door, you need to try this on for size /

The Nazarene, AKA Jesus Christ, was God visiting Earth in human form / and he could be easily identified by the many miracles he performed / but although he healed the sick and fed the poor and raised the dead / these were all just a warm up act for the most important things He said /

Jesus asked the people (and by extension you and I) / to follow Him and be obedient to God's commandments and to comply / with the most important twenty percent i.e. love your neighbour as yourself and love the Lord in all you do / but it was impossible for any of us to always live up to those demands / in fact we all fell short and that's called sin but God knew it beforehand / and he knows sin separates the entire world and takes us out of his hold / so he had to make a plan to ensure we were all brought back into the fold /

and that was why He stepped into time to be the final sacrifice / that would bring us back to him so for us he paid the ultimate price / and although he was innocent he came to die a criminal's death / being punished in your place and mine and even at his final breath / he said "forgive them all 'cos they don't know what they do" / while the collective weight of our unrighteousness was tearing him in two / but he stayed nailed up on that piece of wood to see the matter through /

and although he died in agony he still had us on his mind / but the matter didn't end there because when they laid him in the ground / no-one guessed what would happen next as they left without a sound / but less than three days later just as Jesus Christ had claimed / he rose up from the dead even though no-one could survived the injuries he had sustained /

and he walked around and told his friends that everything was okay / and that the kingdom of God had come and was already underway /

and he continued to regale them with the message of the truth / and he showed his nail prints and his scars to those who demanded proof / Then he ascended into heaven and here's the bottom line / If you believe that he died in your place and all your sins he took away by his grace / and undeservedly he delivered you from disgrace / and for you has prepared an honoured place in glory by his side /

then he will act as your insurance policy against any legal claim / that the enemy of your soul might orchestrate to drop you any blame / because the kingdom of God has no blame culture and plays no games of shame / and your destiny will be to live forever in his kingdom and in his name /

I've given you the clues
You've heard the good news
Now you have to choose
Will you win or lose?

What is your destiny?

Suffer, Little Children

Tiny new born baby
Lying on the bed
Would you really like to grow up
If you knew what lay ahead
Was income tax
Scourge of the poor
Overpopulation
And the threat of war
Terrorism, climate change
Crashes on the stock exchange
Poverty and the search for peace
Atrocities beyond belief
People lying to each other
Rarely honest too much bother

Tiny new born baby
I hope you'll never know
Too many trials and torments
That often lay us low
But I suspect that just like us
You'll see your share of sorrows

My prayer is that you'll find the one
Who holds all our tomorrows

I pray you'll find great joy in life
I pray that you'll find love
But most importantly I pray
You'll find faith in Him above

Tiny new born baby
Sleeping in your cot
Don't grow up to be like us
You're something we are not
Stay just as you are today
Don't let the hate wash you away
Your life is precious pure and new
Heaven's made of ones like you

Matthew 19:14

Credo

I don't believe in miracles
Like rising from the dead
I don't believe in people
Who can conjure fish and bread
I don't believe in people
Who say they've found the truth
I don't believe in anything
Unless I see the proof

I don't believe in viruses
And I don't believe in germs
And I don't believe in God
Because we're not on speaking terms
I believe in nothing
Less it's something I can see
There's only one thing I believe in
I believe in me

I don't believe in yesterday
I don't believe tomorrow
I don't believe in happiness
I don't believe in sorrow
I don't believe the papers

And I don't believe the news

There's no such thing as a third world
And people without shoes

I don't believe in homelessness
I don't believe in hell
And I don't believe in heaven
It's just a story that they tell

I don't believe in love
'Cos it's something I can't see
There's only one thing I believe in
I believe in me

No, I don't believe in God
'Cos he doesn't talk to me
There's only one thing I believe in

I believe in me

When Revival Comes

When revival comes

    Opticians will have their eyes opened
Electricians will see the light
Surgeons will open their hearts
Doctors will be healed
and midwives will be delivered

When revival comes

    gardeners will turn over a new leaf
sanitary workers will be cleansed
ice cream sellers will ring the changes
and traffic wardens will feel just fine

When revival comes

    goalkeepers will be saved
cricketers will be bowled over
boxers will be knocked out
rugby players will be converted
and golfers will be made whole

When revival comes

     judges will be convicted
     juries will make decisions
     and inmates will be released

     policemen will see the evidence
     teachers will know the truth
     and politicians will speak it

This is what will happen
     when revival comes

Acts 2:17

Protection

I don't wear no body armour, I don't wear no Kevlar suits, I don't need no riot shield, got no need for steel capped boots. I got no need of a crash helmet or a health insurance plan 'cos I got a personal bodyguard who protects me where I am.

I found it right there written in the 23rd Psalm where God says it's a certainty that I ain't gonna come to any harm. He's gonna lead me to a peaceful place to where I can experience the fullness of His grace. He's planning me a banquet where I can eat for free right there in the presence of my enemy there's a table that's set aside just for me and that's the best place anyone could possibly wanna be.

The waters run still and the waters run deep and I got no need to worry got no reason to weep, 'cos in these troubled times He is my personal life guide and I can walk with confidence through dark places with Him at my side.

He can call on weapons they are awesome in their power He's the most effective body guard you could shout for at any hour and His armaments are lethal and He packs a mighty punch and if you think you can stand against Him then you're really out to lunch.

You see He'll fight for His people and He'll never let us down and if anyone stands against us he'll put them in the ground He's the champion of the universe He'll keep us safe and sound He's my Father, He's my king, He's my best friend when I'm down, He's my saviour, He's my healer, He's the source of my salvation, He's coming back to fight for us and that's cause for celebration.

Now check this out:

I don't need no more protection
He's my threat detection
He alone is my selection
He is my harm deflection
His strength is my perfection
He got all the muscle flexion
and He leads me in the right direction
'cos He is the resurrection.

Psalm 23

When the clock stops

God always keeps his promises, no shade of turning, no checking of His stride but there's one pledge He has yet to fulfil and one event He has yet to provide and it won't matter if you're still living or by then you have died nothing will stop His long awaited return to meet His Bride.

On that fateful day when He comes back to claim it all, the people of the Earth will assemble to take a curtain call; and as their startled eyes gaze upward and they fear for their eternal souls, their disbelieving eyes will see the darkening skies unroll like the cryptic words inscribed upon an ancient parchment roll.

When He halts the passing of the hours and the minutes petrify He will usher in an era in which none of us will die, where time no longer rules us and space will divide and the people of this planet will gasp in awe and cry as they bow in desperate worship before the Crucified.

Now I am not a prophet or some kind of a holy man but I tell you this with confidence, not everyone will stand because the books will all be opened and the records will be read and only those whose names are found will be saved just like He has said, and there will be no distinction between the living and the dead.

So when time is called on time, and the last days are declared and the presidents and princes of this world stand unprepared, and the Ancient One returns with incomparable power to cause the earth and seas to quake and the mountain ranges cower; then you'll know the truth from fiction and your enemy from your friend, but there will be no more time left for choices, 'cos time will have reached an end.

Then those who truly belong to Him and who are each called by His Name will meet to stand before His throne absolved of any blame. They're the ones who pledged allegiance while time was ticking on, and the ones who turned from darkness to follow the Son. They're the ones who chose to follow and who to their own selves died, they're the people who believed in Him – the redeemed – AKA His Bride.

One day that clock will stop as surely as you read these words I place before you as a warning you should heed, but before the end of days arrives you have a choice to make, I hope you won't ignore this message because for your own sake Christ died for your future, and your eternity is at stake.

Cedars

Giant boughs stretch their sinews out and
upward reach with might into canopies to
punctuate the earth and sky with majestic height
and green ambition soaring in the shimmering
air.

Cedars of the Lebanon grow strong in groves
their giant roots clenched deeply into the rocks
and soil thrusting ancient shoots downwards into
bowels of the earth as constant as God's promises
declared.

Bark and dendrites gnarled and pinched with
age, their foliage offering cool cover like an
ancient cloak for wizened sage, these trees have
sustained for what seems like an eternity
unmovable in their design.

Cedars of the Lebanon give picture of the power
His love affords that reaches deep and high and
wider than a threefold chord that will not break
nor move but stands forever despite the tides of
time.

Signed, Sealed, Delivered

My last blank page
    My last chance
        To tell the world
            To speak the good news
                To inform humankind
                    Of the greatest gift to

                All of them
            All of us
        You and me
      All from Him

    Signed
Sealed
    Delivered

        That's what I am

        John 3:16

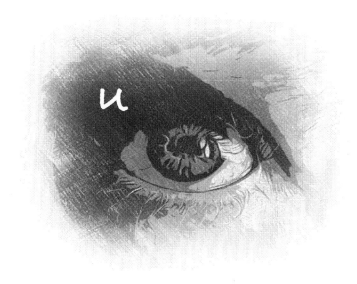

Photo and Image Credits

If you enjoyed this book, you may also enjoy reading two other titles recently published by Wheelsong Books:

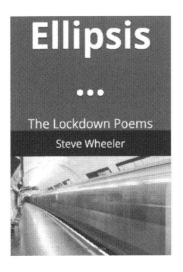

Ellipsis – The Lockdown Poems by Steve Wheeler

ISBN: 9-798666-415252

Poems written during the global pandemic of 2020 with themes ranging from heroism, depression, hope, racism and faith.

Inspirations – Poems and reflections by Kenneth Wheeler

ISBN: 9-798667-258360

Inspiration writing about faith, love, family, life and celebration of all things good. Proceeds go to Open Doors charity.

Both titles are available to purchase in paperback and Kindle formats on Amazon.

Printed in Great Britain
by Amazon